## ROBERT HOLMAN

Robert Holman was born in 1952 and brought up on a farm in
North Yorkshire. He was awarded an Arts Council Writers'
Bursary in 1974, and since then has spent periods as resident
dramatist with the National Theatre and with the Royal
Shakespeare Company in Stratford-upon-Avon. His plays,
including *The Natural Cause*, *German Skerries* (for which he
won the George Devine Award), *Other Worlds*, *Today*, *Making
Noise Quietly*, *Across Oka*, *Rafts and Dreams*, *Bad Weather* and
*Holes in the Skin* have been seen in cities as far apart as Los
Angeles and Tokyo, following their premieres at such theatres
as the Royal Court, The Bush, the RSC and Chichester Festival
Theatre. He has also written a novel, *The Amish Landscape*.

Robert Holman

# JONAH AND OTTO

**NICK HERN BOOKS**
London
www.nickhernbooks.co.uk

**A Nick Hern Book**

*Jonah and Otto* first published in Great Britain as a paperback original in 2008 by Nick Hern Books Limited, 14 Larden Road, London W3 7ST

*Jonah and Otto* copyright © 2008 Robert Holman

Robert Holman has asserted his right to be identified as the author of this work

Cover image by Jorge Tutor, www.jorgetutor.com
Cover designed by Ned Hoste, 2H

Typeset by Nick Hern Books, London
Printed and bound in Great Britain by CPI Antony Rowe, Chippenham, Wiltshire

A CIP catalogue record for this book is available from the British Library

ISBN    978 1 85459 554 6

*Jonah and Otto* was first performed in The Studio at the Royal Exchange Theatre, Manchester, on 12 March 2008, with the following cast:

OTTO BANISTER     Ian McDiarmid
JONAH TEALE       Andrew Sheridan

*Director*   Clare Lizzimore
*Designer*   Paul Burgess
*Lighting Designer*   Kay Harding
*Sound Designer*   Claire Windsor

*To Matthew Holman*
*who will have to read it when he's older*

**Characters**

OTTO BANISTER

JONAH TEALE


*The play is set on the East Sussex coast in the present day.*


*There is one interval.*


*This text went to press before the end of rehearsals and so may differ slightly from the play as performed.*

## ACT ONE

### Scene One

*A secluded public garden in a seaside town on the south coast of England.*

*A brick wall with a heavy wooden door in it. The door is shut. An ornamental lamp-post, to one side, doesn't quite reach the height of the wall. The light is on.*

*A summer night with a full moon. It is bright.*

OTTO BANISTER *is feeling the warmth of the wall with the palms of his hands. There is something sensual about the way he touches the bricks. He is 62. He is wearing a baggy, black suit and a grey shirt, open at the collar. The size of the wall makes him seem small and insignificant.*

JONAH TEALE *enters slowly and stops by the lamp-post. He is 26. He has slightly dirty fingernails. He is wearing jeans and a T-shirt with a worn, corduroy jacket. He watches intently.*

*It takes* OTTO *a while to realise someone is there.*

OTTO. So what if I am. So what if I do feel lonely. I'm not saying that I do.

*A slight pause.*

So what if I am all sorts of things. I expect it's what you're thinking. It's your eyes that are giving you away.

OTTO *stops. He is embarrassed. He puts his hands deep into his trouser pockets.*

So what if I am peculiar. I don't care a jot. The point about having no friends is that you also have no enemies.

*He feels the wall with the palms of his hands.*

The bricks absorb the heat of the summer's day, young man, and give it back to you at night. So what if you are a smart-arsed kid. Yes?

JONAH. I didn't say a thing.

OTTO *stops and looks at him.*

OTTO. I think you were about to.

JONAH. Was I? I wasn't about to say anything, grubby imbecile.

JONAH *takes hold of the lamp-post, leans out and swings round in a full circle.*

You know the furry stuff on your tongue after a disco? Is your brain full of it?

*He swings round again. He comes to a halt.*

I'm ridiculously worried, old man. I'm stony-broke, to be honest with you. My pockets are ridiculously empty.

OTTO *thinks for a second.*

OTTO. No. Not from me. I will not be bullied by a hoodlum like you.

JONAH. I need a bank raid of it, snotty-nose.

OTTO *leans back against the wall.*

OTTO. You must know you can hurt me. I can't possibly stop you. I won't give you money. You'll have to hurt me for it.

JONAH. I can predict the future, but only when I know what's going to happen.

*The town-hall clock, nearby, strikes midnight.* JONAH *swings round the lamp-post once more. On the twelfth stroke he stops.*

Only a little joke.

OTTO. Is it?

JONAH *smiles.*

JONAH. It could be in your heart to give us something.

OTTO. Why?

JONAH. It would be kindness, wouldn't it?

OTTO. I'm not kind.

JONAH. I know. I can tell.

OTTO. I've no money on me at the moment.

JONAH. You've mountains of money. It's coming out like you've got a sweat on. I can stink it from here.

*He goes to* OTTO. OTTO *flinches. He puts his hand in* OTTO's *jacket pocket and brings out a fifty-pence coin. He holds it on the flat of his hand.*

Mister. See?

*He throws the coin high into the air, and catches it by his own pocket so that it almost drops straight in.*

It's a disgrace to be poor. Is it my bloody fault?

*He runs his hands down* OTTO's *jacket.* OTTO *flinches. Unseen, he palms* OTTO's *wallet. He holds out the flat of his hand where there is a fifty-pence coin.*

You know what you are, piggy-wiggy?

OTTO. I expect you're about to tell me.

JONAH. You're a money box. You're full of sour grapes. I don't bet you are. I know you are. Is it my fault?

JONAH *throws the coin into the air and catches it by his pocket so that it drops straight in. He moves away. He takes off his jacket. Almost without looking he hangs it on a tiny, unseen nail in the wall. The jacket seems to hang in the air. He goes to the lamp-post. On the way he looks in the wallet. He pockets the money. He takes hold of the lamp-post and swings round.*

You know what else?

OTTO. Tell me.

JONAH. You're a worm with a worm's-eye view.

OTTO. How would you know what I am?

JONAH. I'm a fabulous guesser.

> JONAH *goes towards* OTTO. *He has a pack of playing cards tied with a rubber band. The band comes off. He shuffles the deck. He fans them.*

Pick a card.

OTTO. What?

JONAH. Pick a card. Take a card.

OTTO. Why?

JONAH. Take a card.

> OTTO *hesitates.*

Humour me.

> OTTO *takes a card.*

Tell me if it's not the seven of clubs.

> OTTO *looks at the card. He has the seven of clubs.* JONAH *fans the deck.*

Put it back, old man.

> OTTO *puts the card back in the pack.* JONAH *ties them with the rubber band and puts them in his pocket.*

What's your favourite card?

OTTO. I don't have a favourite card.

> JONAH *takes a pack of playing cards from his pocket and takes off the rubber band.*

JONAH. Is your imagination in your cock? That's no imagination at all. Pretend I'm a pretty girl.

> JONAH *shuffles the deck.*

OTTO. The king of diamonds.

JONAH. Hold these.

> OTTO *takes the cards from him.*

Where is it?

OTTO *looks through the pack.*

JONAH *moves along the wall. He begins to remove a single brick that is loose.*

You're going to miss it.

OTTO *joins him. The brick is out.* OTTO *puts his hand in the hole and finds a playing card. He holds it up.*

OTTO. The king of diamonds.

JONAH. Is your brain full of dandruff?

OTTO. What?

JONAH. Your eyes need a hospital appointment.

OTTO *looks in the hole. He finds his wallet.* JONAH *takes a hundred pounds in notes from his pocket. He fans the notes like he did the playing cards.*

Are you in anguish, old man? You'll tell me if I've not entertained you. I bet it's been worth every single penny?

OTTO. You need to work on your patter, young man.

JONAH. It's my birthday. July the tenth. It's minutes old. It's a present. Thank you.

OTTO. Why didn't you ask? All you had to do was ask me.

JONAH. Can I keep it?

OTTO. No.

JONAH. I told you.

OTTO. You've a choice now.

*A slight pause.*

If I was you I'd make the right choice.

JONAH. What does that mean? You're a creepy-crawly on a lettuce leaf.

OTTO. It's not a dilemma. You know what it means.

JONAH. Do I? I don't.

OTTO. I think so.

   JONAH *looks down. He looks back up.*

JONAH. Fuck off. Shitbag. Cunt. Who cares.

OTTO. In a small way I believe you do.

JONAH. Do I?

OTTO. I would guess so, yes.

JONAH. What makes yer think that?

OTTO. I'll leave you to tell me.

JONAH. You've lost me already.

   *A slight pause.*

   Sod off.

OTTO. No.

JONAH. Make the world a better place. Go and chuck yourself off the pier.

OTTO. No.

   JONAH *gives the money to* OTTO. OTTO *offers him the king of diamonds with a ten-pound note.*

   Happy birthday.

JONAH. Why? Not now.

OTTO. Take it.

JONAH. Why?

OTTO. Take it.

JONAH. I can't. You'll make us feel bad really. I can feel terrible for weeks. I can be upset for months.

OTTO. Take it.

JONAH. I've told you.

   JONAH *takes the king of diamonds but not the money. He starts to go.*

OTTO. Swindler. Young trickster.

JONAH. Who?

OTTO. You heard me. Has someone got the better of you at last?

*JONAH stops. He takes a small kitchen knife from his pocket. He turns and points the knife at OTTO.*

JONAH. If I see you again, I'll fuckin' kill you. It's a fucking promise.

OTTO *takes a step back.*

*JONAH takes a deck of playing cards from his pocket and throws them high into the air. The playing cards flutter down all around him.*

I'll riddle your heart. No fucking joke.

JONAH *exits.*

OTTO *is still. He puts the money in his wallet and the wallet in his pocket. He bends down with his hands on his knees and takes a deep breath.*

*JONAH enters. He is pushing a supermarket trolley. One wheel is slightly larger than the others so that the trolley moves up and down unevenly, and one wheel squeaks. In it is a rucksack, a sleeping bag, and a carefully constructed bed for a baby. The baby's face cannot be seen because of the bedding she is surrounded by.*

OTTO *looks up.* JONAH *stops.*

Are you waiting for a bus?

OTTO *is astonished.*

OTTO. What?

JONAH. Mister. Thanks a lot for the tenner.

OTTO. You didn't take it.

JONAH. I will in the end, I promise. I get hot and bothered and het up sometimes. It's nothing much. She's asleep.

OTTO. What?

JONAH. Come and see.

OTTO. Who?

JONAH. Come and see a miracle.

OTTO *goes to the trolley.*

OTTO. Is she your child?

JONAH. Yeah. She's very beautiful, isn't she?

OTTO. You left her on her own?

JONAH. Only for a few minutes. I was worrying all the time.

OTTO *takes his wallet from his pocket and gives* JONAH *a ten-pound note.*

I'll pay you back.

OTTO. You won't. There's no need. It's only money.

JONAH. I will. I absolutely promise. I'd pay you back now, but then I wouldn't have it.

OTTO *is exasperated.*

OTTO. Why did you have to find me?

JONAH. Pardon?

OTTO *goes away towards the wall.*

OTTO. You can't go on like this, young man.

JONAH. Like what?

OTTO *turns to him.*

OTTO. I don't know you. You're the one who knows you.

JONAH. I don't go on. I'm just me. A bit daft. I'm an entertainer.

OTTO. It isn't just you.

JONAH. It is.

OTTO. It isn't.

JONAH. Oh.

OTTO. No, it's not just you.

OTTO *takes thirty pounds from his wallet. He goes to*
JONAH *and gives him it.*

JONAH. I'm not an egg. You're not an egg. Sure as eggs is
eggs, I'll see you get it back.

OTTO. You won't.

JONAH. I definitely will.

*He puts the money in his pocket.*

Shall I tell you something?

OTTO. No.

JONAH. You're amazingly, stupendously brilliant.

OTTO. I'm not. I can only wish that I was sometimes.

OTTO *goes away to the wall. He feels the warmth of the
bricks with the palms of his hands.*

JONAH. It's a bit fuckin' peculiar, is that.

OTTO. Is it? Yes, I expect it is, if you say so.

JONAH. You want to watch out. You're more peculiar than I
thought. You'll end up stuck in a fantastic rut.

OTTO. Everything is a narcotic. I love a good wall. There's
something sweet about loneliness. I had promises to keep. I
failed miserably. Life? It's just one more thing to keep clean.

*He stops.*

I'm thinking aloud. Are you still here?

JONAH. What does it look like, smelly-pants.

OTTO. I don't know you. I don't like you. I don't want to know
you, and I certainly don't want to like you.

*He takes a packet of low-tar cigarettes, in a white box, from
his jacket pocket.*

JONAH *is watching him.*

Yes?

JONAH. Nothing. It's a free country, or it was yesterday when I
looked.

OTTO *lights a cigarette with a match.*

You've a syphilitic tongue, and that's a fact.

OTTO. I crave affection. That's the deepest need I have and it's true of everyone. Is it true of you?

OTTO *throws the match away. He smokes in an unusual fashion. He holds the cigarette, halfway down its length, between his thumb and forefinger.*

JONAH. You talk gobbledegook.

OTTO. Do I now?

JONAH. I've just said so. You talk shit.

OTTO. Of course you're completely right, as always.

*A slight pause.*

Perhaps it's this. Perhaps there's more to you than meets the eye.

JONAH *takes an apple from his pocket. He begins to peel it with the kitchen knife.*

I won't be ridiculed. I won't be messed around by a young hoodlum like you.

JONAH. Who says I'm a hoodlum?

OTTO. I judge as I find.

JONAH. I'm not a hoodlum.

OTTO. I don't know you.

JONAH. If you're going to judge as you find, you'd better be right.

*A slight pause.*

OTTO. You've disturbed my peaceful evening. I ought to be thankful, but I'm not. Young reprobate.

JONAH. Pardon?

OTTO. I think you heard me.

JONAH. Be rude.

OTTO. I'm right. I can afford to be rude.

*JONAH has peeled the apple in a circle so that the peel is in one long piece. He holds it up and starts to eat it from one end.*

Spit it out.

JONAH. It's my apple. Get lost.

OTTO. The venom. The anger.

*A slight pause.*

You're making me anxious. I don't know why. I thought you might ask me why.

*A slight pause.*

Life is bloody terrifying sometimes.

OTTO *raises his voice.*

My hostilities are me. I am my hostilities. I can't help it.

*A slight pause.*

Your silence is making me anxious.

*He goes towards JONAH.*

Of course I feel bloody sorry for myself. Doesn't everyone?

JONAH. Bog off.

OTTO. I will.

*JONAH kneels down. He takes a white handkerchief from his pocket. He spreads it on the ground. He starts to cut the apple into quarter pieces.*

JONAH. Go and tell the drip-drip of your life to someone else.

OTTO. I will.

*JONAH puts the apple and the knife on the handkerchief. He cuts out the core of each quarter of apple before starting to eat it.*

JONAH. Go and jump off a cliff. Walk along to Beachy Head and be brave with yourself.

OTTO. I will.

*JONAH is still. He stands up. He adjusts the baby's covers in the trolley.*

JONAH. The thing is, my best mate topped himself. Actually, it's not funny. He was only thirteen.

*He looks at* OTTO.

He had a mop of black hair and a face like a bucket. I used to call him Bucket Head.

*He bends down.*

Piece of apple?

OTTO *puts out the cigarette. He takes a quarter piece of apple from* JONAH. JONAH *is standing.*

His parents were posh.

*He moves one of his fingers in a tiny circle.*

They used to peel apples like that. I didn't think of it until now.

*A slight pause.*

That's it. That's all. Except I loved him.

*A slight pause.*

I was a mucky. We were poshies and muckies. A mucky kid. I wasn't a smart-arsed kid, by the way. I'd too many problems for that.

*A slight pause.*

Least said, soonest mended. Give over looking at us.

*He looks away, shyly.*

Yer like a steamroller with yer eyes.

*He looks at* OTTO.

You must know what it's like to love someone.

OTTO. Yes.

JONAH *looks away.*

JONAH. I don't. Except for Bucket Head, that is.

*He looks at* OTTO.

He hung himself. In the bedroom. With the light on. One Sunday night. He couldn't face school. I hope he could face me. I don't know. We were just kids. Me scruffy. Bucket Head in his smart blazer. The fuckin' bastards who used to belt him, I could fuckin' belt them now.

*A slight pause.*

I used to scruffy him up. We swapped clothes once, just to see what would happen. Nothing. No difference. He used the cord off his pyjamas. Old-fashioned. They were old-fashioned, Mr and Mrs Bucket Head. I had elastic. He'd have used the sheets on the bed, I suppose. Tiny. He was tiny. I mean, I was small, but he was ridiculous.

*A slight pause.*

He told me he was going to do it. I was thirteen. It fuckin' hurts. You know what hurts the most? Mr and Mrs Bucket Head gave me his toys. His Scalextric. His magic box. He had a dressing-up kit, with some girls' knickers in. I even played with those.

*A slight pause.*

The thing is, I didn't know him. As I put the knickers on, I knew there was more to it. They were white. He'd cut a little hole in one of them.

*A slight pause.*

I took them to school. I showed everyone. I put my finger through the little hole and I wiggled it. I can't forgive myself. I can't find an excuse for that. There is no absolution.

JONAH *smiles*.

I'll break your legs if you don't shut up.

OTTO *turns away slightly. He hopes his hands won't be seen. He takes a handkerchief from his pocket and wipes his fingers on it. He wraps the apple in the handkerchief and puts it in his pocket.*

JONAH *bends down and picks up a piece of apple. He offers it to* OTTO.

OTTO. You're a mischief-maker. There are demons in you, young man.

JONAH *eats the piece of apple in one go. He kneels. He cuts out the core of the last piece of apple. He puts it between his teeth. He takes hold of the handkerchief and tips the apple cores onto the ground. He puts the knife and the handkerchief into his pocket. He gets up. He eats the apple.*

JONAH. What would you think if we was the last two people on earth?

OTTO. I'd think how unlucky I was to end up with you.

JONAH *smiles.*

JONAH. Yer cracked.

OTTO. If you say so.

JONAH. Yeah, I do. I mean it an' all. Someone should put you down, end the misery. Go and do euthanasia on yourself.

OTTO *is looking at him.* JONAH *looks away, shyly.*

Give over.

OTTO. What?

JONAH. Looking at us.

OTTO. No.

JONAH. Give over.

OTTO. No.

JONAH *looks at* OTTO.

JONAH. Don't give over then. See if I care.

JONAH *looks away.*

OTTO. I'd think how lucky I was.

JONAH. Bog off.

OTTO *smiles.*

OTTO. Don't you like it?

JONAH. What?

OTTO. Being appreciated.

JONAH. Bog off.

*A slight pause.*

OTTO. Use your big man's knife. Go on. Be tough.

*A slight pause.*

Exactly.

JONAH. Take a staple gun to your lips and have a party with it.
You go on like you've got an itch in your crutch all the time.

*Silence.*

OTTO. You are very, very shy, aren't you?

JONAH*'s shoulders go up. He covers his head with one of
his arms. It is a contorted position. It is as if he has been hit
and is unable to defend himself.*

I am so, so sorry.

JONAH. Just leave us alone. It's my life. What I am's got
nothing to do with you.

OTTO *goes to touch him.* JONAH*'s hand comes out to fend
him off. His head starts to twitch very slightly.*

I can't help it. I get panicked.

JONAH*'s body closes in on itself. He is getting smaller all
the time. He battles for the words.*

I want to go away and hide. When it gets like this I don't
know what to do.

JONAH *takes a breath. He finds oxygen. His body is
twitching very quietly.*

It happened when I was a kid. It's the worst feeling in the
whole wide world.

OTTO. I am sorry.

JONAH. I can't fight back.

JONAH *battles for the words*.

I haven't the confidence. You shouldn't see us like this. It'll go in a minute.

*A slight pause.*

I know I'm useless.

*A slight pause.*

I'm worthless.

*A slight pause.*

I'm very small.

*He wipes some of the sweat off his forehead and face with the back of his hand. He is still.*

OTTO *takes his handkerchief from his pocket. He remembers the apple is inside. He unfolds it and holds the top corners so that the apple drops to the ground.*

OTTO. Here.

JONAH *shakes his head*.

JONAH. Why?

OTTO. Take it.

JONAH *shakes his head*.

JONAH. Why?

OTTO *folds the handkerchief in half and in half again. He puts it on the ground by* JONAH. *He goes away to the wall. He leans back on it. His arms are by his side, and his palms are touching the bricks.*

OTTO. I can only apologise profusely.

JONAH *looks at him*.

JONAH. Is that it, old man?

OTTO. Yes.

JONAH. Yer nothing but a piece of gob. To be honest with you, yer not even the gob. You're nothing.

OTTO *smiles*.

You're a herbert.

OTTO. What's a herbert?

JONAH. Just a herbert, weasel's breath.

OTTO *smiles*.

OTTO. Is this part of your act?

JONAH. What's that when it's at home? You're a slug surrounded by salt.

OTTO. The patter. You know.

JONAH. Yeah, I go round the pubs trying to earn an honest penny. So what? What's it to you?

OTTO. With your cards and your tricks?

JONAH. Yeah.

JONAH *picks up the handkerchief. He unfolds it. He is holding a white mouse by the tail.*

What's this if it's not a fantastic trick?

## Scene Two

*Open ground on the way to Beachy Head.*

*The earth rises slightly. There is a rickety fence made of thin, triangular pieces of wood held together by lengths of wire. Within it are a couple of palm trees that have grown twisted in one direction because of the wind. This helps to give the fence the aura of something once meant to be temporary. Behind the fence is the sea, which cannot be seen or heard, and the sky, which can be seen and fills everything. The sky dominates the earth.*

*There is a backless wooden bench. It is little more than a piece of wood on two supports in the ground. It has been weathered by rain, by the salt in the air, and by generations of people sitting on it.*

*A few hours later. Already there are traces of blue in the pale dawn of the sky.*

JONAH *enters, pushing the trolley. He goes some way towards the bench before stopping. He goes to it and sits. He waits a moment before taking off his jacket. He folds it in half and puts it on the bench beside him.*

OTTO *enters. He goes straight to* JONAH. *He has a packet of cigarettes.*

OTTO. Happy birthday. Again.

JONAH. I might not smoke, grubby dimwit. Weasel's stomach. Lousy bloody scum.

OTTO. You're a smoker.

> JONAH *takes the packet.* OTTO *walks away. He stops and looks at the view inland.*

JONAH. What are you then, if you're ever honest with yourself?

OTTO. I'm a smoker, too, but rather more half-heartedly.

JONAH. That's not what I meant.

OTTO. I know it isn't what you meant, it's the answer I'm giving you.

JONAH. You're a remarkable man. Am I to blame?

> JONAH *puts the cigarettes on top of his jacket.*

I know what ambiguity is, you're bloody full of it.

> OTTO *turns to him.*

OTTO. Guess. If you're such a good guesser.

JONAH. What are you going to pay me?

OTTO. A tenner.

> OTTO *takes a ten-pound note from his wallet.*

JONAH. Your face doesn't quite fit. Something along those lines.

OTTO. I'm giving you a tenner for that?

JONAH. I haven't finished yet.

OTTO. It had better be good.

JONAH. It will be.

*A slight pause.*

You're unhappy, so I reckon that makes you a little bit moral.

*A slight pause.*

OTTO. Yes, that is worth a tenner.

*He goes to the bench. He sits. He puts the ten-pound note on top of the jacket.*

JONAH. You put your money on the wrong horse. All your life I would guess.

OTTO. And I thought you were a smart-arsed kid.

JONAH. I bet you buy your own underwear. Only lonely men do that.

OTTO. Are you going to offer me a cigarette or what?

JONAH. No.

OTTO. I'll have to smoke my own then.

*He takes his packet of cigarettes from his jacket pocket. He offers one to* JONAH. JONAH *accepts and takes a Clipper lighter from his pocket. He lights both his and* OTTO's *cigarettes.*

JONAH. These are hardly worth the bother.

OTTO. They're ultra-mild. Like me.

JONAH. They're shit.

*JONAH stubs out the cigarette on the side of the bench. He puts his elbow on his knee and rests his head on his hand and looks at* OTTO *in a deliberate way.*

OTTO. I'm a nonentity, young man. I even fear losing that.

*A slight pause.*

What?

JONAH. You do it to me.

JONAH *continues to look at him.*

OTTO. I didn't embarrass you.

JONAH. Now you know what it feels like.

OTTO *looks away.*

Twinkle-toes.

OTTO. What?

JONAH. Look at me.

OTTO *looks at him.*

OTTO. You are too charming for your own good.

JONAH. Fairy-feet.

OTTO. I'm married. I've four daughters who at best tolerate me. I don't know how old you are.

JONAH. You're not going to know.

OTTO. Well, they're adults, like you. They're not children any more.

JONAH *continues to sit in the same position.*

I went to Cambridge. I'm not a council-house hoodlum.

JONAH. That's a judgement.

OTTO. Yes, it is, and meant. I studied philosophy and theology.

JONAH. Big words.

OTTO. Small words. Big ideas. I became a clergyman. I am a clergyman. You are embarrassing me for some reason.

*He picks up the ten-pound note.*

I'm taking this back since you didn't guess I'm a clergyman.

JONAH *snatches it out of* OTTO's *hand.*

JONAH. Not on your nelly. I need it. It's mine. I've a baby to feed.

*He smiles. He puts the note in his pocket.*

I wouldn't be talking to you if it wasn't for the money, don't you fret.

OTTO *stubs out his cigarette. He stands up. He walks away.*

Are you going somewhere pleasant for the day with yourself?

OTTO *stops. He turns.*

OTTO. Why are you so aggressive?

JONAH. Far as I'm aware, I owe you nothing. So keep your mental comments to yourself.

OTTO. It's stuck on your face. In your bad mouth. Your eyes say something else.

JONAH. You've said that before.

OTTO. I meant it before. You've a conscience. Listen to it. It whispers, but it's there all the same all the time.

JONAH *looks down.*

JONAH. Who cares.

OTTO. You most certainly do.

JONAH *looks up. He smiles.*

JONAH. Don't make yourself at home. You're not stopping.

OTTO. You are bloody disarming.

JONAH. What's that mean?

OTTO. You know what it means.

JONAH. Do I? I wish I did. I might be more brainy.

*A slight pause.*

Cotton-socks.

OTTO. Yes. Go on. Be rude.

JONAH. Whereabouts are you a clergyman and stuff?

OTTO. Here. I'm waiting.

JONAH. It's a dump of a place. It's no wonder yer bonkers.

OTTO. Yes, I expected nothing else.

JONAH. It's all buckets and spades.

OTTO. Is it?

JONAH. It's all families on a day out, pretending to be happy. It's candyfloss.

OTTO. Did you try the pier?

JONAH. Yeah, I did, since you ask.

OTTO. Were you unceremoniously turfed off?

JONAH. Yes, I was, since you want to know.

OTTO. I've grown into the place. Or the place has grown into me. I've been here for eighteen years.

JONAH. It's the pox.

OTTO. Of course you're right.

JONAH. I am. Poxy seaside towns. I hate them all.

*A slight pause.*

OTTO *sits down. He spreads his legs flat on the ground and leans back on his hands.*

*A pause.*

JONAH *gets up. He goes to the trolley. He adjusts the baby's covers. He sits down near* OTTO. *He spreads his legs on the ground and leans back on his hands.*

*A pause.*

The thing is, I don't mean it really.

OTTO. I know.

JONAH. I know you know. It's why I do it. It's my shyness. You were right the first time.

*A pause.*

JONAH *gets up. He goes to the trolley. He opens the ruck-sack and takes out a ragged, paperback copy of* Verse and Worse. *He lies down near* OTTO. *He has his back to* OTTO. *He rests his head in his hand and reads some poetry.*

*A pause.*

JONAH *shuts the book. He turns to look at* OTTO.

D'you believe in God?

*A slight pause.*

OTTO. No.

*A slight pause.*

Are you asking out of politeness or malice?

*A slight pause.*

JONAH. It spells trouble, if you ask me.

OTTO. Yes.

*A slight pause.*

I haven't believed in God for a long time. Perhaps because I haven't believed in myself for a long time. It did leave me feeling very lonely. You must think I'm a fool.

JONAH. Yes.

OTTO. Gullible.

JONAH. Yes.

OTTO. Sad.

JONAH. No, I wouldn't say sad.

OTTO *smiles.* JONAH *smiles.*

Are you still doing it all the time?

OTTO. Doing what, might I ask, young man?

JONAH. Saying prayers and what not?

OTTO. Yes.

JONAH. I didn't mean the other.

OTTO. I know you didn't. God may forgive your lies, eventually.

*A slight pause.*

JONAH. Did God do something to you?

OTTO *smiles.*

OTTO. Yes, He did. He came along when I wasn't watching. He rather caught me off my guard. When I was a young boy. I was a rather too gentle teenager. On holiday with my parents in Cornwall. I was smitten by the Lord. It was like being in love for the first time. It was joyous.

*He looks at* JONAH. JONAH *lies back and looks at the sky.*

You know about love.

*A slight pause.*

Your friend at school.

*A slight pause.*

There were a group of teenagers singing hymns on the beach, in Polperro. I was sixteen. One girl, a very pretty girl, invited me in. I was going to be an architect, or a painter. A single moment of being asked to join in changed my life.

*A pause.*

JONAH. I am listening.

*A slight pause.*

OTTO. She was awfully pretty. I ought to have known it was wrong because the first thing I did was go away and pleasure myself.

JONAH *leans on his elbow and looks at* OTTO.

JONAH. What? Have a wank?

OTTO. Yes.

JONAH. How pretty?

OTTO. Pretty beyond any of my dreams these days.

JONAH. I'd have had two wanks.

> OTTO *smiles, chuckles slightly.*

> Were you a grammar-school boy?

OTTO. I wasn't comprehensive scum, like you. I was a true-blue posh person.

JONAH. You don't mean that.

OTTO. Don't I? I do.

JONAH. You're copying us really.

OTTO. Am I?

> JONAH *looks down. He finds his book. He reads.*

> *The light is still coming up. The pale colours of the dawn are beginning to be replaced by the blue of the day.*

> OTTO *looks at his watch.*

> I'm going to have to go in a minute. I've a service to take. It may be your birthday, but it's also Sunday.

> JONAH *sits up, cross-legged.*

JONAH. Can I ask you something else?

OTTO. Yes.

> *A pause.*

JONAH. It's this really. Have you ever loved anyone else apart from God?

> OTTO *smiles.*

> That says it all really.

OTTO. What?

JONAH. The fact that you didn't say anything.

OTTO. The answer is yes.

JONAH. Who?

> *A slight pause.*

> You see.

OTTO. I'm thinking. It isn't easy. It's a very personal question.

JONAH. I know it isn't me.

OTTO. Well, I don't know you.

JONAH. You do.

OTTO. Do I?

JONAH *looks down.*

I've always loved God in a very different way to the women I've loved. Of course that's so. I believed in God's love. God's love for me. He caught my eye. I wasn't quick enough to look away. The women I've loved, I perused. I've sought their attentions for very different reasons.

*A slight pause.*

I'm not sure I want to say. Except it must be obvious to you. If you ask me have I been faithful to my wife, the answer is no. My brain loves a pretty girl. It always has, so it always will.

*The white vapour trail of an aeroplane can be seen moving across the sky.*

I later married the girl I met on the sands in Polperro.

JONAH *looks at him.*

I was a young curate in Liverpool. I know something of poverty, and anger, and despair. I know low spirits. I've a doctorate, in divinity. I liked to think I'd an intelligence about the world. It didn't help me in front of a pretty girl. That's my sadness, in this beautiful yet terrifying world.

*A slight pause.*

Do I believe in God? No. Because God doesn't believe in me.

OTTO *wipes a single tear from his eye with the corner of his thumb.*

If there are no tears when I speak, there'll be no tears when you listen. It's not a tear, anyway. It's just a scratch.

*He takes his wallet from his pocket. He offers* JONAH *a twenty-pound note.* JONAH *hesitates, then takes it. He puts the money in his pocket.*

I believe in art, in great paintings. And poetry. I believe in the
power of the human spirit. And friendship, when it's possible.

JONAH *looks away.*

I believe in God as a supreme reality. God as expressed
through the people we meet, whether we liked them or not,
whether they like us or not, whether we can be helpful.

*A slight pause.*

And I believe in guilt. But you know about that already.
Don't you?

*A slight pause.*

Don't you?

JONAH. Yes.

*Church bells begin to ring out in the far distance.*

OTTO. I believe in you.

JONAH. I'm not worth it.

OTTO. Yes, you are.

JONAH. I'm not.

OTTO. Yes, you are.

JONAH. I wish.

OTTO. Yes, you are.

JONAH *looks up.*

JONAH. Why?

OTTO. I'll leave that up to you. You decide.

OTTO *gets to his feet. He exits.*

*A long pause.*

JONAH *takes the money* OTTO *has given him from his
pockets. He takes a large bundle of notes, tied with a rubber
band, from his back pocket. The rubber band comes off. He
puts the money together. He fastens it with the rubber band.*

**Scene Three**

*The open ground.*

*A few hours later. The day is almost still, the sky an azure blue.
The heat of the day is attracting the occasional cloud, which
drifts off.*

JONAH *is sitting at one end of the bench. He is feeding the
baby with a bottle. On the rest of the bench is his jacket, baby
clothes, a bottle of water, a sterilising unit, more babies bottles,
measuring spoons, milk powder, a portable gas ring, a small
pan, a nappy-changing pad, nappies, baby wipes, cotton wool
and a small teddy bear. It all looks new and shines in the sun. At
the opposite end to* JONAH *is a dirty nappy, folded together,
and the empty rucksack.*

OTTO *enters. He is dressed in the same suit and shirt, but the
top button is now fastened and hidden behind a clerical collar.
He stops. He looks at* JONAH.

JONAH *takes the bottle from the baby's mouth and holds it
up to see how much she has drunk. He feeds his daughter,
calmly.*

OTTO *goes to the bench. He takes hold of the dirty nappy and
the rucksack and puts them on the ground. He sits. He watches
for a moment.*

OTTO. How old is she?

JONAH. Six weeks.

    *A pause.*

OTTO. You make me feel nervous.

    JONAH's *attention is on his daughter.*

JONAH. Why?

    *A slight pause.*

OTTO. You fill me up with anxious hypothesis because I really
    want to know you.

*JONAH takes the bottle from the baby's mouth. The milk has gone down a little. He feeds his daughter.*

JONAH. You do know me.

OTTO. No. Not at all. Not in the least.

*A pause.*

JONAH. I love her tiny fingers. All the tendons and nerves inside. Amazing. They're beautiful.

*A pause.*

You won't change me. Not really.

*A pause.*

I love all her little body. Amazing vulnerable.

*A black-headed gull is not far away. It calls and cackles for a moment. It flies off.*

We've looked at the sea. She has a wanderlust. Don't you?

*A slight pause.*

She'll not settle for second best.

*He holds up the bottle. The bottle is half-full. He feeds his daughter.*

OTTO. What did you study at university?

JONAH. Books. English. How did you know?

OTTO. A guess.

*A slight pause.*

Where?

JONAH. Hull.

*A slight pause.*

OTTO. Who's hurt you?

JONAH. I beg your pardon?

OTTO. Who has hurt you?

JONAH. No one.

OTTO. Someone has.

*A slight pause.*

OTTO *gets up. He walks away a short distance. He looks at the view inland. He goes to the bench and sits. He smiles.*

I go and I come back. It's the story of my life.

*A slight pause.*

Your family?

JONAH. Please don't.

OTTO. So it's them.

*A pause.*

My father was German. It explains why my name is Teutonic.

JONAH. I don't know your name.

OTTO. Otto. He took my mother's maiden name when they married. I was born in 1946. He was a doctor, my dad. He was very much against the military of all kinds. My mum was a teacher. In Manchester. I can hear her in you. We ended up in Berkshire when I was just old enough to remember the move, but that's another story.

*A slight pause.*

I'm an only child. Are you?

*A slight pause.*

JONAH. I've a brother and sister.

OTTO. Every year we'd go to Polperro. I'd get the bus on my own to St Ives, to see Barbara Hepworth. A very sexy woman. She'd make me a cup of tea. A stringy fourteen-year-old with a long scarf, even in summer. I was far too naïve and innocent for my own good. Yet a little bit randy at the same time.

*A slight pause.*

Don't you know about art?

JONAH. Should I?

OTTO. Yes.

JONAH. I don't.

OTTO. Fucking ignoramus.

*A slight pause.*

JONAH. I've no say over my age. I can't go and see her when she's dead.

*A slight pause.*

Did you fancy her really?

OTTO. In my wet dreams.

*A slight pause.*

JONAH. Knutsford. Is where I'm from. I went to Knutsford High School. It's not a crummy comprehensive, by the way.

OTTO. In Manchester?

JONAH. Cheshire. Nearby.

*A slight pause.*

I used to cream my jeans over a girl in our class. Denise Morgan. She was a right bloody looker.

OTTO. Rumpy-pumpy?

JONAH. Yeah.

*A slight pause.*

I didn't. I was too quiet.

OTTO. I went to a boys' school.

JONAH. Rumpy-pumpy?

OTTO *smiles*.

OTTO. No. I was starved of pretty girls from a young age.

JONAH. You've been making up for it ever since, sounds like.

*A slight pause.*

OTTO. You did well at school. You must have done rather well.

JONAH. No.

*A slight pause.*

They're your Achilles heel.

*A slight pause.*

Do I need to dot the i's and cross the t's?

OTTO. Chastity is very unnatural. Unfortunately for me, sin is addictive.

*JONAH holds up the bottle. It is nearly empty. He feeds his daughter.*

JONAH. Your wife?

OTTO. Don't be catty.

JONAH. Was I going to be?

OTTO. I'm not sure about you.

*A slight pause.*

JONAH. I bet there's no rumpy-pumpy there.

*A slight pause.*

OTTO. That would be me telling you too much, if I haven't already.

*JONAH takes the bottle from the baby's mouth. It is empty. He puts it on the bench.*

JONAH. She's asleep.

OTTO. Of course you're right. It's a sham. It's to keep up appearances. Yet I still couldn't live without her.

JONAH. She can live without you, and that's a true fact. Is it?

*OTTO thinks for a second.*

OTTO. Of course you're perfectly right.

*JONAH gets up. He puts the baby carefully in the trolley. He adjusts her shawl. He closes his eyes and looks at the sun.*

JONAH. I hope she'll do more than tolerate me.

OTTO. What?

JONAH. You said your daughters tolerate you. I hope she'll do more.

*He puts a blanket over the end of the trolley to create some shade. He looks at the view inland.*

Have you a son?

OTTO. No.

JONAH. You want a son.

OTTO. Yes.

*JONAH sits. He spreads his legs flat on the ground and leans back on his hands. He closes his eyes and looks at the sun.*

*Silence.*

JONAH. They think you've got turn-ups on your underpants.

OTTO. Who?

JONAH. Your daughters.

OTTO. I'm sure you know best.

JONAH. I do know best. I've known best a long time.

OTTO. Is this another part of your act?

JONAH. Yeah.

*A slight pause.*

OTTO. Did you finish your degree?

JONAH. Fuck off.

OTTO. You must be known in the pubs in Hull.

*A slight pause.*

JONAH. The thing is, I only care about myself, to be honest with you. Dad.

OTTO. Fuck off.

*Silence.*

What?

JONAH. I've fucked off.

*A pause.*

You used to know a lot. Then what happened? You got
older. You worry too much. Your brain's a rubbish heap.
This is part of my act, to be straightforward with you. If
God doesn't care twopence, why should I? You think you
know about character. You know fuck. I wasn't bothered in
the first place. I care less than an old shilling about what
you think. You hang around. You take liberties. Yer worse
than my cock the way you want loving. The way you
riddle me with your sympathy. You're like a fucking
machine gun. No one loves you, old man. You use your
loneliness like a weapon. It makes a noise. It pleads. It
shouts out.

JONAH *opens his eyes. He looks at* OTTO.

The truth is important sometimes. There's some kind of truth
you want me to see. I'm just giving you it back.

OTTO *closes his eyes.*

You're not my dad. You're someone who means money.

OTTO *opens his eyes.*

You want to know me. It scurries up and down you like a
disease. Jesus knows why. I thought you were gay, for about
ten minutes. A secret stash of boy-porn in the wifely home. I
did enjoy the thought, for about ten minutes. Why do you
want to know me?

OTTO *closes his eyes.*

Mister. Otto. The thing is, it's a vital question. Is it for me, or
is it for you? Is it for my sake, or is it for your sake?

OTTO *slowly opens his eyes.*

OTTO. Your sake. My sake. They're the same thing when two
people are friends. I can only tell you what I think I've said
before. D'you want to hear it?

JONAH. No.

OTTO. Good. Very fine. Hunky-dory. I'll sit here and wait for
your insecurity to say yes.

*A slight pause.*

JONAH. And a day went by, said the big brown bear to the little
brown bear.

*A pause.*

Yes.

OTTO. Look somewhere else before I say it.

*JONAH looks away.*

There is something about you that cries out to be loved. I
understand that. But that's not my point. You, young whip-
persnapper, are worth loving.

*A slight pause.*

I've got turn-ups on my underpants. It's very old-fashioned,
isn't it? End of sermon. It's better than the one I've just
delivered, to be straightforward with you. Fuck the Church.
Fuck Jesus. Fuck God. I'm interested in you.

*OTTO closes his eyes.*

I know you are no concern of me. I understand that as well.
But you want to know me, too.

*He opens his eyes.*

Yes, you do. We can go round and round in circles. Or we
can move on.

JONAH. I thought you were dying.

OTTO. What?

JONAH. You keep closing your eyes. I asked my mum once:
can you die with your eyes open? I was ten. When I was
eleven, I asked Bucket Head if he thought you could. It was
a bit precipitous really. I used to worry I'd be alive when
they put me in the ground. I've a brain like the skin on a
chicken. It has a seizure now and again. I'm away with the
birds when my brain goes. My mum said you couldn't die

like that. Bucket Head said you could. I used to worry about
my pills. A red one and a yellow one in different bottles.
Bucket Head said I should think of them as Smarties so I'd
want to take them. He said my brain made me unique. He
said to me: I wish I was you. We were twelve. I went home
and I thought about both those things. I lay quietly on the
bed. I did my breathing to help stop a seizure. I thought if I
worked hard at school maybe I would learn something. Even
go to university like my big brother. My mum said: it's possible, Jonah. She used to worry about me. To start off with, I
got my worries from her. Then slowly they belonged to me.
They became mine. When I was thirteen, she said to me:
everything is possible, Jonah, look at Richard, he's an architect. We were walking back from Bucket Head's funeral.
She'd come with me. I thought I owed it to Bucket Head to
be private. I was thinking a lot about that in any case. I
wanted to be private. Then the birds would come in. My
head would go funny. I'd get the taste. I'd go the colour of
liver. I'd hear a scream hit my lungs. My mum would say:
it's all right, Jonah, it's over. She'd make tea. Something
incredibly special to get rid of the taste. She'd worry about
money. We weren't rich. And do without things for herself.
She'd say to me, secretly: you were always my favourite
boy. She'd smell my clothes before she washed them. She'd
have washed me if I'd let her. She wanted me to be young, to
make me easier to deal with, as well as there being that little
thing between mother and boy. I was fourteen by then and
having none of it. The Smarties went. They were people. In
my imagination they were teachers, parents and policemen.
They could go fuck themselves. I set fire to the house. Just
for the joy of it. I didn't want to be liked. I watched it burn. I
saw the flames lick the roof. The fuckin' taste of the smoke
in my mouth, like I'm dying, like I'm always dying before a
seizure. It was fantastic. It was fucking thrilling. It was,
beyond doubt, the best day of my life so far. The thing is, I
had an outburst of temper. I was fifteen. I'd try to talk to
girls, then my tolerance would snap. They'd want to know
me. They'd want to know about my lousy brain. That's what
it felt like. I wasn't about to tell them fuck. I'd go furious
again. A secret isn't a secret unless you keep it. Something

like that. I don't know why really, except I was lonely, I said
to Denise Morgan: will you masturbate me? And she did.
Though my cock was in my trousers. I was close to coming
anyway. It took five seconds. The brush of her fingers along
my crutch was enough. She knew what to do. It was in the
school corridor. It was break time. Boys pushing. A crush of
people. I've always been really alone with people there.
Their eyes were like spears. I thought of Bucket Head and
the hole in the girls' knickers, and I thought I knew him a
little bit better. It was raining. An English autumn day as it is
always described in books. The clouds like a roof on the
world. I looked at the boys. I thought to myself: you don't
know me, you never will know me, you are never going to
know a thing about me. They were laughing. Denise Morgan
was smiling. And the birds came into my head. I was sixteen.
I learnt to write it down. To try to be objective. I wanted to
understand. Not a boy. Not a man. Just me really, just Jonah.

OTTO *closes then opens his eyes.*

JONAH *gets up. He looks at his daughter. He moves the
trolley slightly so that the blanket will continue to provide
her with shade. He looks at* OTTO.

She's very good the way she sleeps. You go to sleep if you
want.

OTTO *closes his eyes. He drops asleep on the backless
bench. He is balanced, somewhat precariously, in a more-or-
less upright position, slightly leaning on one hand.*

JONAH *looks at him for a moment. He goes there. He
brushes open* OTTO*'s jacket and carefully takes a small
notebook from one of the inside pockets. He flicks through
the pages looking to see what is there, stopping to read the
odd thing or two. He carefully tears a page from the notebook, folds it in half, and puts it in the back pocket of his
jeans. The notebook goes back into* OTTO*'s jacket.* JONAH
*continues the search. He takes* OTTO*'s wallet from the other
inside pocket. He looks at the money that is still there. He
takes a ten-pound note, puts it in the back pocket of his
jeans, and returns the wallet to* OTTO*'s pocket.* JONAH
*stops. He looks at* OTTO *for a moment.*

JONAH *bends down. He takes off one of* OTTO'*s black shoes and looks at it. He puts it against his own shoe, trainers which were once white but are now ragged and falling apart, and judges it for size. He takes off his trainer. He puts on* OTTO'*s polished black shoe, fits his foot into it, looks at it, judges it and walks about a few paces as if he was in a shoe shop. He decides the shoe is good and fastens the laces. It's time to see if he likes both shoes and if they are a good fit. He takes off* OTTO'*s other shoe, puts it on, ties the laces. He walks about. The shoes are good. He bends down. He puts his old trainers on* OTTO'*s feet and fastens the laces.*

JONAH *stands. He looks at* OTTO, *at his grey shirt and the white clerical collar. He looks at his own T-shirt. He decides* OTTO'*s shirt is better and starts to unbutton it. The clerical collar comes off.* OTTO *is wearing a white vest.* JONAH *manoeuvres the shirt off without taking off* OTTO'*s jacket. He is a magician. The shirt comes off down the sleeve of* OTTO'*s jacket.* JONAH *takes off his T-shirt. He puts on* OTTO'*s shirt, buttons it, and tucks it in. He looks at* OTTO'*s trousers. He looks at his jeans. He takes the piece of paper and the money from the back pocket of his jeans, and puts it on top of the nappies on the bench.*

JONAH *bends down. He undoes* OTTO'*s belt and the catch on his trousers. He undoes the zip. He tickles* OTTO'*s chin.* OTTO *moves slightly, enabling* JONAH *to pull down one side of* OTTO'*s trousers. He tickles* OTTO'*s chin.* OTTO *moves the other way, enabling* JONAH *to take down the trousers all the way.* OTTO *is wearing pale-blue boxer shorts.* JONAH *takes off* OTTO'*s trainers. He takes off* OTTO'*s trousers. He puts the trainers back on* OTTO'*s feet, but this time does not fasten the laces.* JONAH *takes off his jeans. He puts on* OTTO'*s trousers and fastens the belt. He picks up the piece of paper and the money and puts them in the back pocket of his trousers.*

JONAH *looks at* OTTO. *He takes off* OTTO'*s jacket. He puts it on. He picks up his jeans. He finds the rest of the money, the knife and the cigarette lighter. He puts them in the pockets of his new trousers.*

JONAH *sees* OTTO*'s watch. He undoes the strap and puts it on his own wrist.*

JONAH *sees the clerical collar. He fastens it round* OTTO*'s neck.*

JONAH *picks up the corduroy jacket on the bench. He drops it on top of the other clothes on the ground. Perhaps he allows himself a faint smile.*

JONAH *takes the cigarettes from his jacket pocket. He takes one, tears off the cork tip, and lights it with a match.*

JONAH *smokes.*

*End of Act One.*

## ACT TWO

### Scene One

*The open ground.*

*A long enough time has gone by for* JONAH *to have smoked the cigarette. He takes a last drag and puts it out by nipping it with his fingers and standing on it with his shoe. He picks up the empty rucksack by the sleeping* OTTO's *feet and begins to fill it with the baby things on the bench. The sterilising unit goes in first, followed by everything else. It all goes in, somehow. All that is left is the dirty nappy which goes in a side pocket. He takes the rucksack to the supermarket trolley and his daughter. He puts it on the ground and kneels down to fasten the catches.*

*The air is still. There is not a breath of wind blowing off the sea.*

JONAH *goes still. He stares. It is as if the day has gone and he is absent from it.*

JONAH's *head jerks. The pupils in his eyes roll up. He is on the ground. His muscles tighten. The air is forced out of his lungs. He cries out as the air goes. His teeth clench as his jaw muscles contract. He stops breathing for a moment. He goes blue. He is sweating. He is dribbling. A thick saliva is coming out of his mouth.*

JONAH's *leg starts to twitch. It is slight at first but grows in intensity. His arm and trunk muscles convulse. His whole body begins to shake rhythmically. His limbs thrash the ground. He is beating hell into the earth. His body is jerking and twitching and moving. He quietens down. The whole thing has gone on for less than a minute, though a minute is a long time.*

JONAH *returns to consciousness.*

*Silence. Stillness.*

JONAH *slowly moves his hand to his trousers to see if he has wet himself. He is lucky this time.*

*Silence. Stillness.*

JONAH *curls round to double-check the front of his trousers with his eyes.*

*A pause.*

*He reaches out for the rucksack. He undoes a side pocket. Out of the pocket comes a Smarties box. He takes some tablets, still in the protective wrapping, from the box. He presses two tablets through the foil. The tablets are different colours. He swallows them. The rest of the tablets go in the Smarties box and the box in the rucksack.*

*Silence. Stillness.*

JONAH *takes a white handkerchief from his pocket. He spits some spit from his mouth into it. He gets more comfortable. He sits. He wipes round his mouth and face. He spits more spit into the handkerchief.*

*The white vapour trail of an aeroplane can be seen moving across the sky. It is coming back the other way from a few hours ago.*

JONAH *wipes across his teeth with his thumb. He wipes his thumb on the handkerchief. He continues to clean his teeth. He puts the handkerchief away. He takes an orange from his pocket. He peels it with his fingers. He puts a segment in his mouth and sucks on it.*

OTTO *slowly opens his eyes. He sees what he is wearing.*

JONAH *puts another piece of orange in his mouth.*

OTTO. Your insouciance doesn't impress me at all.

　OTTO *stands up.* JONAH *looks at him.*

JONAH. Why not?

OTTO. You are incorrigible.

*He waves his hand through the air in a dismissive gesture.*

JONAH. Temper, temper.

OTTO. You're unpardonable. May God have you rot in hell. I wash my hands of you.

OTTO *sits on the bench.*

JONAH. You're cracked. You care too much.

OTTO. What about?

JONAH. You tell me.

OTTO. What?

JONAH. I said, you tell me.

OTTO *stands. He is still waking up. He puts his hand on the bench to steady himself. He raises his voice.*

OTTO. I won't tell you anything.

JONAH *raises his voice.*

JONAH. Stop shouting. Wind your neck in.

*A slight pause.*

I've got a headache. Just bloody stop shouting. Have a piece of orange.

*He holds out a piece.*

OTTO. No.

OTTO *sits. He takes the clerical collar from his neck and throws it down onto the bench.*

Little shit.

JONAH. I beg your pardon?

OTTO. You heard me.

JONAH *eats a piece of orange.*

Headache gone?

JONAH. Nearly.

OTTO. You didn't have a headache.

JONAH. I do still, to be honest with you.

*A slight pause.*

OTTO. Little cunt.

JONAH. Naughty, naughty. Naughty language. Liverpool's tongue.

OTTO. Yes.

*A slight pause.*

JONAH. I couldn't care less really.

OTTO. Couldn't you? Couldn't you?

JONAH. No.

OTTO. I like you. Would you like to know why?

JONAH. No. I don't give a fuck.

OTTO. That's why I like you. You're such a liar.

JONAH *sucks a piece of orange.*

You're a disgrace to yourself, to me, to everyone.

JONAH. I told you not to shout.

OTTO. Fuck off.

*A slight pause.*

Little bastard.

JONAH. Head for the gutter. Guttersnipe. See if I care.

OTTO. Yes, you do care. I know you care.

*A slight pause.*

JONAH. Who is arsed about you, old man?

OTTO *gets up. He goes towards* JONAH. *He stops.*

OTTO. You don't know me.

JONAH. I know enough for you to hang around.

OTTO. What?

JONAH. I said, I know enough for you to hang around me. You could be a million other places.

OTTO. Yes.

JONAH. Go on then.

OTTO. What?

JONAH. Hang around someplace else.

OTTO. No.

JONAH. I've given up hinting.

OTTO. I don't care what you think.

JONAH. I wasn't bothered in the first place.

> JONAH *gets up. He sits on the bench.* OTTO *watches him.*

> God doesn't like you. Why should I?

> JONAH *eats some orange.*

> You've made yourself comfortable with me.

OTTO. Yes, I have.

> *A slight pause.*

> I don't know how much I love people. Do you?

JONAH. I don't know. I don't care really.

OTTO. You keep on saying that.

JONAH. I keep on meaning it.

> *A slight pause.*

> I could have said I haven't a fucking clue. I could have said yes. I said I don't know.

> OTTO *sits. He spreads his legs flat on the ground and leans back on his hands.*

> You weren't listening when I told you, you were going to sleep.

OTTO. I was listening.

> JONAH *takes his handkerchief from his pocket. He spreads it on the bench. He puts what is left of the orange on top of it.*

> OTTO *looks at him.*

> JONAH *is embarrassed. He sort of shuffles and plays with his hands. He swings round on the bench and looks the other way.*

JONAH. I'm on my own. I'm me, myself, and I. I don't need anybody.

OTTO. Don't you?

JONAH. I've just said really.

OTTO. Yes.

JONAH. I don't need you the most.

OTTO. You know how to be unkind. I've come to need you.

OTTO *gets up. He sits on the bench and faces the other way to* JONAH.

JONAH. You always add stuff, kind of thing. You always make it worse.

OTTO. What?

JONAH. Me. You always make me feel worse.

OTTO. Do I?

JONAH. Another bloody question that's not really a question but a bloody fucking comment.

OTTO. Is it?

*A slight pause.*

JONAH. I'm out for a good time really.

OTTO. The discos in the town know you well.

JONAH. I don't go to discos.

*A slight pause.*

Why are you happier always talking about me?

*A slight pause.*

OTTO. I'm shy, actually. I'm shy of you. I'm somewhat frightened you won't like me.

*A slight pause.*

JONAH. Enjoy the afternoon. Enjoy the sun. Stop worrying.

JONAH *swings his legs round. He plays with the orange with his finger, breaking it up, squashing it. He then flicks away some little bits of fruit with his finger.*

I can't give you what you want.

OTTO. What do I want?

JONAH. Love. It's not within me.

OTTO. Love is terrifying.

JONAH *stops. He wipes the length of his finger along the handkerchief on the bench.*

That took courage, didn't it?

JONAH. Yes.

OTTO. You're very hidden.

*A slight pause.*

JONAH. You're bonkers.

*A slight pause.*

OTTO. I must be telling you I don't like myself very much. Am I?

JONAH *smiles.*

JONAH. I know you don't.

*A slight pause.*

The world is silent. We all hate ourselves, in my opinion.

JONAH *plays with the fruit with his finger.*

OTTO. I want to get to know people for fear of being lonely, and then I want to get rid of them because they know me too well.

*A slight pause.*

All the people I've loved have made me laugh. You've absolutely no sense of humour.

JONAH *smiles.*

You don't know a woman until you've fucked her. I've tried to know far too many women.

JONAH. Piffle and tosh. Twaddle and claptrap.

OTTO. You're contemptible. You've no backbone.

JONAH. Who's the liar now? You wouldn't know honesty if it gave you a good slapping.

*JONAH flicks some fruit in* OTTO's *direction.*

OTTO. How's your headache?

JONAH. I have a headache all the time. Don't worry about it.

*He flicks fruit in* OTTO's *direction.*

OTTO. Stop it.

*JONAH stops.* OTTO *wipes some fruit off his leg.*

*There is a shy silence between them.*

Where is the baby's mother?

JONAH. Fuck off.

OTTO. It's that bad.

JONAH. You know shit.

*JONAH smiles.*

OTTO. What about your mother?

*A slight pause.*

Your dad?

*There is shyness between them.*

JONAH. You're my dad.

OTTO. Fuck off.

*JONAH takes the box of matches from his pocket. He cleans beneath his fingernails with a match.*

JONAH. There's nothing to say really. He climbed the ladder to heaven when I was a child.

OTTO. Yes.

JONAH. Why d'you want to know so much?

OTTO. It's my job.

JONAH. Fuck off.

OTTO. It is my job to be sympathetic.

JONAH *flicks the match. It flies off somewhere.*

JONAH. He got cancer. He had bowel cancer. He farted a lot, then he passed away. All in about nine months. I was only nine. Nines are everywhere. That's the other thing I had to have done. I had to have a colonoscopy. I wouldn't have minded really, but all the students had to look up my bum as well.

OTTO *smiles.*

It's not funny.

OTTO *chuckles.*

OTTO. Did you love him?

JONAH. Yeah. I did. He was the best dad in the world.

*There is shyness between them.*

OTTO. D'you still miss him?

JONAH. Yeah. All the time.

OTTO. He misses you.

JONAH. Fuck off.

OTTO. He does.

JONAH. I wish he did.

OTTO. He does.

*A slight pause.*

JONAH. D'you really think so?

OTTO. Yes.

*A slight pause.*

JONAH. Yer just make us feel bad again.

OTTO. Good.

JONAH. Bastard.

*There is shyness between them.*

He was only forty-six. I missed him like hell. I used to go to my mum, and try and be good an' that. I used to really try. I used to bake. To be extremely honest with you, I could make cakes and stuff. I used to do little butterfly buns with a Smartie on top as an extra. She did her best to cover up. I wish she hadn't really. I wish we'd all sat down and cried. My mum had two miscarriages between my brother Richard and me. It's why he's a bit older. I don't know why I'm telling you this. Except it made a difference really. My mum told me what it was like to lose two children. So I always felt a bit responsible. I always felt I had to try really hard. You said there must be something funny in the family. There isn't. My sister's at college. She's going to be a doctor. The only thing that's funny is that I'm the thick one. And my mum. She teaches infants. She works hard for us all. I do my best not to be private with her. Except I am a touch. I wasn't as a boy. It just got that way as I grew up. I know it hurts her a little bit when I don't say much sometimes. I do try. I think you have to have one of your parents pass away, for you to sit down and talk to the other one. The trouble is, my dad passed away when I was too young for it to be possible. I hate him for that. I don't. I hate him for dying. I'd know my mum better if he hadn't died. It's odd. It should be the opposite. It isn't.

JONAH *and* OTTO *are looking at one another.*

*A pause.*

You've a little red patch over your eye.

OTTO. Where?

JONAH *touches his own eye.*

JONAH. Just here. It's tiny.

OTTO *rubs his eye.* JONAH *looks again.*

It's not a stigmata. It's a touch of eczema. You must sleep with one eye open.

OTTO. What does that mean?

JONAH. It means nothing.

*There is shyness between them.*

JONAH *looks at his watch.*

OTTO. What time is it?

JONAH. That would be telling.

OTTO. Cunt.

*The sun is just beginning to go down. The sky is turning deep blue, and any clouds are a memory. In a short while the earth will know the power of the evening.*

Thank you.

JONAH. Stop worrying.

OTTO. Do I worry?

JONAH. Yeah.

OTTO. Will I worry myself into a grave?

JONAH. You already have. You can't do nothing about yourself.

OTTO. What does that mean?

JONAH. It means you can't do nothing about yourself. You have to accept it. You're a fucker. You're a naughty boy. You cover the world with dirt.

OTTO. You'll make me insecure in a minute.

JONAH. No. You're insecure already.

OTTO *looks away.*

OTTO. Cunt.

JONAH *smiles.*

JONAH. You're chuckling really. You love it. Being the centre of my attention.

OTTO. I most certainly am not.

JONAH. Yes, you are.

OTTO *looks at him.*

OTTO. Yes, I am.

JONAH. I told you.

OTTO. Yes, you did.

*There is a powerful shyness between them.*

I'm frightened.

JONAH. I know.

OTTO. I'm frightened of life.

JONAH. I know.

OTTO. Cunt. I'm frightened of death. I'm frightened of God.
I'm frightened of you. I'm frightened I'll do it all wrong. I'm
frightened I've done it all wrong.

JONAH. What?

OTTO. God's work. The work He has asked me to do. I've
done it wrong.

*A slight pause.*

JONAH. No.

OTTO. Yes.

JONAH. I promise you.

OTTO. Cunt.

*A slight pause.*

JONAH. I bet you love it. I bet you love hating yourself. Fuck it
and fuck you, is all I can say.

OTTO. What makes you so wise?

JONAH. Nothing. You're full of self-pity. It hangs off you like
a coat.

OTTO. Stop.

JONAH. I won't stop.

OTTO. Enough. End. Finish.

*There is silence between them.*

JONAH. God likes you, by the way. D'you want to know why?

OTTO. No.

JONAH. God likes you because I like you, and I'm in touch
with God.

   OTTO *looks at him.*

OTTO. Where d'you get all this from?

JONAH. I fuckin' hurt. That's where I get it from.

OTTO. I know.

JONAH. Why ask then?

   *There is silence between them.*

   God loves you. Because I love you.

   OTTO *shouts.*

OTTO. Stop it.

   OTTO *gets up. He walks away. He looks at the view inland.*

   Fucking cunt. Little shit.

   JONAH *swipes at the handkerchief and orange, and they go
   flying onto the ground. He lies back, flat on the bench.*

   Little runt. Little bastard.

   JONAH *takes a mouth organ from his pocket. He half plays
   a song by The Beatles and half makes a noise.*

   OTTO *waves his hand through the air in a dismissive
   gesture. He walks somewhere else.*

   *A slight pause.*

   OTTO *finds himself looking at the baby.*

   You don't talk to her at all.

   JONAH *plays loudly.* OTTO *shouts.*

   You don't talk to your daughter.

JONAH *plays loudly. He stops.*

JONAH. She's asleep.

OTTO. No, she's not. She's awake.

JONAH. She'll cry when she wants me.

JONAH *plays the mouth organ. He stops.*

OTTO. I didn't mean to upset you.

JONAH. You haven't. Stop worrying.

*He puts the mouth organ in his pocket.* OTTO *goes to him.*

OTTO. You're trembling.

JONAH. You've seen it before. What you on about?

OTTO. Why?

JONAH. I've told you why. I go tiny sometimes.

OTTO. You're sweating.

JONAH. You want to get your memory sorted out. I wasn't being honest with you. I was being extremely honest. I'm just nervous. Leave us alone.

OTTO. Nervous of what?

JONAH. Everything. I want to die. I want to be with my dad.

*He battles for the words.*

I've still never cried for my dad. I'm a big man.

*A slight pause.*

OTTO. I'm sorry.

JONAH. I was really trying.

OTTO. I know you were.

JONAH. It's how I get with my mum. I'm useless. It has no end. It just comes and comes and comes.

*A pause.*

OTTO. Sit up.

JONAH *shakes his head.*

JONAH. No.

OTTO. Sit up.

JONAH *sits up.* OTTO *sits down.*

I didn't cry for my dad. You're not the only one who's useless. I'd give you a hanky but you've gone and ruined it.

JONAH *blows his nose into his hand. He flicks away the mess onto the ground.*

That is disgusting.

JONAH. Yeah.

OTTO. It's no wonder you've mucky fingers.

JONAH *blows his nose again. He flicks away the mess.*

I really and truly didn't cry for my dad. He was a pacifist, so he must have had some passion somewhere within him. I never saw it. Your dad was a passionate man, Jonah. I believe so. I can see him in you. He is within you. That's love. It's love reflected. My dad is nowhere within me. I wish he was. It might somehow make me a better person. But he isn't. I don't have his Germanic reserve. I do have some of his oddness. The little lies that go on behind the closed curtains in every home in the world. The little secrets that betray us eventually. I don't know what in particular I'm trying to say to you.

JONAH. I do.

OTTO. Do you?

JONAH. Yeah, I've just said so.

OTTO *chuckles.*

I knew you'd chuckle.

OTTO. Why?

JONAH *shrugs.*

JONAH. Does there have to be an answer to everything?

OTTO. Yes. There is if you believe in God. I am a mass of con-
fusions, which isn't surprising at my age. Our doubts are our
passions somehow. I don't believe in the shit any longer. The
truth is, I wouldn't care if you were a murderer. I know
you're not, but I wouldn't care. You're an arsonist, a cozener,
and a little bit of a thief. I don't care about the reasons why.
As you've seen, I'm not a reasonable person. Whenever I
look at myself, I get scared. I know you understand that.
That's enough for me to know. I don't believe in the devil. I
wish I did. It would make life easy.

*A slight pause.*

If you weren't here. I'd have to invent you.

*JONAH looks away.*

JONAH. Like people invent God because they need Him?

OTTO. Yes.

*JONAH gets up. He goes to the trolley.*

JONAH. She is awake.

OTTO. You've done nothing to deserve this. I'm sorry.

*JONAH adjusts the baby's covers.*

JONAH. Why?

OTTO. Fear.

JONAH. You make us think a bit. It's bloody scary.

OTTO. Is it?

JONAH. Yeah. I don't know what I might do. What I might be.
What I could be. It's bloody terrifying.

OTTO. Is it?

JONAH. Yeah. I've not shrunk. Have I?

OTTO. No.

JONAH. Have I gone in on myself?

OTTO. No.

JONAH. It makes a change. I usually would have done by now.

JONAH *goes back to the bench. He sits.*

OTTO *looks at the trolley and then at* JONAH.

OTTO. What's she called?

JONAH. Ginny.

OTTO. She needs you to be good.

JONAH. Yeah.

OTTO. Astute. Discerning. Subtle.

JONAH. Yeah, I am. Aren't I?

OTTO. No.

JONAH. Thanks a bunch. Thanks for nothing. Yeah.

*The sun is almost on the horizon. The sky is becoming filled with the red and yellow colours of evening. It will be a magical, painterly sunset that will overwhelm them and yet enhance the small things they are doing.*

The trouble is, I don't like people. She couldn't live on my finger.

OTTO. You don't like people.

JONAH. I've said.

OTTO. You don't trust people.

JONAH *is nervous.*

JONAH. Yeah. Maybe. I mean, I do and I don't. Everything's a do and a don't with me.

OTTO. Where would you rather be at this minute?

JONAH. Somewhere else. I want to be the only person in the world when I get like this. I want to be the only person in the world, full stop.

JONAH *looks away.*

OTTO. Your girlfriend?

JONAH *looks at* OTTO.

JONAH. It's why I'm here really. She's in France. We couldn't get tickets. At Newhaven. To go to Dieppe. She got a ticket. It's stupid. We thought we'd get on. They wouldn't even take Ginny. She isn't on our passports. It was all a mess. It was all last-minute. She just rushed on. We hardly said goodbye. Her father's poorly. We thought we'd take Ginny as well. We thought we'd try to be a family.

OTTO. Calm down. What are you nervous of?

JONAH. You.

*The sky is full of red and yellow.*

OTTO. Have a cigarette.

JONAH. I had one a while ago. I've given up.

OTTO. Can I have one?

*JONAH gives OTTO the cigarettes and matches. OTTO lights a cigarette. He smokes in his distinctive fashion.*

*JONAH smiles.*

JONAH. She's French. My girlfriend is French.

OTTO. Rumpy-pumpy?

JONAH. Yeah. Fantastic rumpy-pumpy. It's the best sex ever. She's no inhibitions. She's very French. She knows where to go and it isn't Paris. We were shameless. There was no stopping her. She's very erogenous. I soon found her sensitive places. I was in paradise for about a year. In a cocoon. I've never done so much shagging before or since. My cock couldn't take it in the end. I thought it was going to drop off.

*JONAH takes some cigarette papers from his pocket.*

I will have a fag.

*OTTO offers him a cigarette. JONAH takes three cigarettes. He puts them on the bench. He starts to join three cigarette papers together. OTTO watches.*

She's called Emilie.

OTTO. Your girlfriend?

JONAH. Who else, thick-head? You'll want to know if I love her. Because you always do. The answer is, no. Or I don't know. She's the best thing in my life at the moment.

*He breaks up the cigarettes and puts the tobacco on the cigarette papers.*

I can't help you. I can't help myself.

*He takes a small packet of cannabis from his pocket.*

What is love? You tell me.

JONAH *laces the tobacco with cannabis.*

OTTO. I know this much, it's in the intervals of love that we learn to be aggressive. I'm not talking about desire.

JONAH. Do I look like a dunderhead?

OTTO. Desire is something else. It can make me say the strangest things. It usually bears no resemblance to what I have in mind.

JONAH. I bet you talk about God when you're rumpy-pumpying.

OTTO *smiles. He chuckles slightly.*

Don't you?

JONAH *rolls the joint.*

OTTO. I think we learn to love by loving, by listening to another person. Love is paying attention.

*He is watching* JONAH. *He puts out his cigarette.*

You won't make my age.

JONAH. Who?

OTTO. You.

JONAH. Why?

JONAH *breaks up the joint with his fingers. The tobacco and cannabis is sprinkled on the ground.*

OTTO. I thought you were going to smoke it?

JONAH. No. I'm paying attention.

OTTO. I was rather hoping you were going to offer me some.

JONAH. No. I'm not.

OTTO. Oh.

JONAH. Satisfied?

OTTO. No.

JONAH. You'll have to be unsatisfied then.

OTTO. Why?

JONAH. You won't love me if you see the birds. Tobacco brings on the birds sometimes.

OTTO. I want to know about these birds, young man.

JONAH *raises his voice.*

JONAH. You know less than a cretin. You know complete crap.

JONAH *becomes shy again.*

Emilie's parents run an amusement park in Le Touquet.

OTTO. I've yet to hear you apologise.

JONAH. Pardon?

JONAH *looks at his watch. He takes a passport and ferry tickets from a pocket in his trousers.*

I've sorted it all out. We're booked on the midnight ferry.

OTTO. I've yet to hear you apologise.

JONAH. What for?

*A slight pause.*

I don't apologise.

OTTO. I've noticed.

*A slight pause.*

JONAH. The thing is, I'm not like this really.

OTTO. You are like this.

JONAH. I'm not.

OTTO. You are.

JONAH. Oh.

*A slight pause.*

I don't mean to be like this. I'll be glad when it's midnight.

JONAH *gets up. He puts the passport and tickets in his pocket. He walks away. He looks at the view inland.*

*The earth is being lit by the setting sun. The sky is a fireball of red and yellow.*

Do you use prostitutes?

OTTO *raises his voice.*

OTTO. What?

JONAH. Who's Miss Kitty?

OTTO. What?

JONAH. I tore a page out of your notebook. It said Miss Kitty and a phone number.

OTTO *stands up.*

OTTO. Give it to me.

JONAH. You've an overactive cock. I bet you go feeling a wall, when you want to feel Miss Kitty.

OTTO *sits.*

All this stuff about keeping your bed open. Or whatever it is you said. Is bollocks. You adore women. They've seldom adored you.

OTTO *raises his voice.*

OTTO. What would you know?

OTTO *stands up.*

Fucking kid.

OTTO *rests his hand on the bench to steady himself.*

JONAH. Yeah. At least I'm trying. It's taking courage, is all this. I'm worried about you. Are you all right?

OTTO. Fuck off.

*OTTO sits.*

JONAH. I'm sorry.

OTTO. Fuck off.

*A slight pause.*

JONAH. I'm sorry because I owe you a lot.

OTTO. You took my money. You took my clothes. You've taken my pride.

JONAH. Yeah. I listened to you though. It was interesting really.

*OTTO stands up. He rests his hand on the bench.*

Are you all right?

OTTO. Yes.

*OTTO straightens up.*

JONAH. I care about you, sort of thing. I know you don't like it. I won't say it again. It's odd. I've not known you a day. I thought you were dying for a minute.

OTTO. No.

JONAH. I don't say this sort of stuff very often.

OTTO. Yes.

JONAH. I don't say it ever. I wouldn't be saying it now, except you've helped us a lot. A great deal, actually. More than you know.

*A slight pause.*

Don't you say owt.

OTTO. I wasn't going to.

JONAH. Good.

*A slight pause.*

I can't think of nothing else. Yes, I can. You're the best thing there is in England.

OTTO. Enough is enough.

JONAH. It's only true.

*A slight pause.*

I was looking to have some fun while I waited for the ferry. You've been great. That's a bit of a lie. The fun bit is a lie. You know something? The world doesn't know what it's got in you.

OTTO *sits.*

It's why the world is mad.

JONAH *goes to the bench. He sits.*

I'm sorry.

OTTO. What for?

JONAH. Being me. I know what you're going to say. Don't ever apologise for being me.

OTTO. I was.

JONAH. I have to at this second. It's to do with my life. That's it. It's done. Thank you.

OTTO *gets up. He walks away. He looks at the view inland.*

*The sky is a mass of colour. It runs in horizontal layers, from green at the bottom, through gold, through pink, through red, to orange at the top.*

*The light of the dying sun is picking out the two people.*

OTTO. There are all sorts of things in our loft, there's a pram up there from when the girls were little. Would any of it help you out?

JONAH. Yes.

OTTO. As is the way with these things that become part of our memories, it was put there and it's stayed there. My children have found no use for it. Your daughter is beautiful. When something that is beautiful is destroyed and made ugly by carelessness, I want to shout out. My eldest daughter was knocked over by a car when she was six. She was running across to the shop to buy one of those sherbet dips with the little strand of liquorice that you can't get any more. You won't remember them, like you won't remember the moon walk, or Martin Luther King, or Aberfan. Forgive me, I'm allowed to be critical after what you've done to me. She is not a girl any more. She is a woman who sits all day, who does nothing but dribble out of the corner of her mouth. She was efflorescent. She was more than my life. When she was born she was everything I had prayed and asked God for. Do you understand why some days I can't tolerate it any more, and why I hate her? As she shuffles to the lavatory, she reminds me of what I could have been. As we manage the odd word or two, I know all too well that I didn't live up to the great things expected of me when I was a boy in Polperro.

JONAH *gets up. He moves closer to* OTTO. *He sits. He spreads his legs flat on the ground and leans back on his hands.*

Are you attacking me?

JONAH. No.

*They are looking at one another without shyness.*

OTTO. I fell in love again, in Liverpool, when I was a young man. I nearly told you earlier, but I didn't have the courage. All my life I've wished courage on me. It hasn't, unfortunately, been within me to be courageous. She completely took me over. You know how it is when you think of little else, and daily thoughts go by the by? There is a kind of punishment in being in love, if you're me. She was shy, like you. She was beautiful, like you. She meant everything to me, like you. And she frightened me, like you. She called upon a sort of honesty that I didn't have, as you do. You ask for honesty, young man. It's very frightening. It's very frightening to me. It's very painful to be honest, to have a friend. It's a very scary thing.

*A slight pause.*

I should have left my wife for this girl, but I didn't. I should have left God for this girl, but I didn't. I should have looked at my daughter, who was in a coma by then, and said: I'm sorry, I'm going. I should have looked at the world and said: I'm in love, fuck off.

*A slight pause.*

And I was always gullible, as you've seen. I didn't want to tiptoe through my life, but I've told you I have. *Könnten Sie mir bitte helfen?* I need your help.

## Scene Two

*The public garden.*

*The brick wall. The light is on in the ornamental lamp-post. There is an apple on the ground.*

*The heavy wooden door opens.*

OTTO *comes through it. He is wearing* JONAH's *clothes, including the jacket. Luckily, they fit him well and he does not look out of place in them.*

*The moon is low and powerful. It is one of those nights when the moon is capable of creating massive shadows.* OTTO *is magnified in shadow on the wall.*

OTTO *sees the apple. He shivers. He picks it up. He calls to the door.*

OTTO. I keep getting déjà vu. There is a sophisticated Christian sense that everything has been observed before and in particular by God's love. It has all happened before. There is someone somewhere who knows what it feels like to be us.

*He bites into the apple.*

There was a very, very pretty girl in Durham who caught my eye. She was busy putting flowers in the church. I asked her one day: will you come and help us with the children? My eldest daughter was fourteen by then, with all the adolescent problems magnified many times. She said: yes. We gave her the boxroom in the attic where I know she was comfortable. The vicarage was hell on both counts. I shouldn't have said, I shouldn't have asked, but I did. I've always gone in head first.

*He eats some apple.*

Of course she didn't share my bed. Of course not. For the most part I have not been sinful, except in my thoughts.

*He eats some apple.*

When my father died, I washed his body. I don't why I did it. It was painful. I must have wanted to see him naked, to know who he was, a little. I couldn't comfort myself, yet I like to think I was good at it with others. He was thin, and brittle like old paper. He was easy to tear. He had a scar on his leg I didn't know he had until then. He had been hurt in some way on his leg, by a bullet perhaps. There were a number of people at his funeral, in Reading. On a sunny day like today. He did have friends, which surprised me. It alarmed me somewhat to see so many people. And there was another pretty girl. Yet another like all the others. She was by his grave. A little tear in her eye. I thought: all these years he's had a mistress, he's had a secret. I absolutely adored him for it, and wanted it to be true. I wished it so, so I could be like him. I wanted life to be acceptable.

*He eats some apple.*

She did come into my bed, eventually. I am acquainted with the night. I'm not innocent, like my child, my daughter. Whatever she wears, she's wearing rags. A careless moment has robbed her of her shape.

OTTO *has finished the apple. He looks for a bin. He puts the apple core on the ground at the bottom of the lamp-post.*

JONAH *comes through the door. He is pushing an old-fashioned pram. It has the hood up. It is in pristine condition.*

JONAH *and the pram are magnified in shadow on the wall.*

What time must you go?

JONAH. Ten o'clock.

OTTO *shuts the wooden door. He walks somewhere. He looks at his wrist but his watch is not there.*

OTTO. When the time comes, will you just go.

JONAH. Yes.

JONAH *takes off his jacket. He hangs it on another, different unseen nail in the wall. The jacket seems to hang in the air. They are apart.*

OTTO. Have you got everything?

JONAH *feels round his pockets.*

JONAH. Yes.

OTTO. Your passport. Don't forget that.

JONAH *feels in his back pocket.*

JONAH. I've got it.

OTTO. Give my love to Emilie.

JONAH. I will.

OTTO. She is beautiful. You must love her.

JONAH. I'll try. I will.

OTTO. *Ich bin dankbar.* I am grateful. Don't be late.

JONAH. I won't.

OTTO. You don't want to miss it.

JONAH. You're worrying.

OTTO. Yes.

JONAH. I'll be fine. Stop worrying. You worry too much.

OTTO. Give Ginny a kiss every day from me.

JONAH. All right.

*Ginny starts to cry. It is a baby's waking-up cry. It is the first time she has made a sound.*

OTTO. That's a shame. I was hoping she'd sleep the journey for you.

*JONAH picks up his daughter. She stops crying. He takes the rucksack from the pram and puts it on the ground. He kneels. He undoes the strap and takes a paperback book from the top.*

JONAH. We've been reading *The Wind in the Willows*. Haven't we?

*He looks at OTTO.*

She's a bit young for it really. I enjoy it. She likes the sound of my voice.

*He puts the book in the pram.*

Don't you, Ginny? Yes, you do. Yes, you do.

*He fastens the straps on the rucksack. He puts it in the pram. He stands up. He looks at OTTO.*

She likes Ratty the best. I like Mr Toad. We argue about it.

OTTO. You've enough nappies?

JONAH. Yes. I'll smack your wrist if you don't stop worrying.

OTTO. Would you like some food to take?

*JONAH gives him a look.*

Yes, yes, yes. Worrying is all I'm good at.

*A slight pause.*

Tell Emilie she has to tell you off now and again. Tell her from me.

JONAH. She tells me off enough as it is.

*The moon is rising. The shadows are getting smaller.*

OTTO *looks at his wrist.*

There's a little while yet.

*He turns so that* OTTO *can see Ginny's face.*

I think she's asleep.

OTTO. She is. She's part of God's world. See she comes to no harm, won't you?

JONAH. Yes.

> JONAH *goes somewhere. He looks at the garden. He looks at* OTTO.

> Would you like to have her for a minute?

OTTO. No. She's yours. I haven't done you a flask.

JONAH. I'll get a cola on the boat.

OTTO. You've done Ginny's bottle?

> JONAH *smiles.*

JONAH. No. I didn't bother with it. I thought I'd let her starve.

> *He goes to* OTTO.

> There's a notebook in my pocket. Here. Can you take it out?

> OTTO *takes a notebook from* JONAH*'s pocket.*

> There's a Biro in my back pocket.

> OTTO *takes a Biro from* JONAH*'s back pocket.* JONAH *takes the Biro off him. He looks at* OTTO.

OTTO. What?

JONAH. Open it and hold it.

> OTTO *opens the notebook at the last entry. He holds it.* JONAH *writes.*

> I write down her bottles, the ounces and the time, in case the birds come, in case I forget.

OTTO. I won't ask about the birds.

JONAH. Good.

> JONAH *takes the notebook and Biro.*

> *'Merci du dérangement.'*

> JONAH *puts them in his pocket. He touches* OTTO*'s eye. It is more or less the first time they have touched. He rubs away a few flakes of* OTTO*'s dry skin.*

You should put some cream on it. I sleep with one eye open because of my fear of dying. It was a weakness, but now it's a strength. It's a kind of humanity. It's a kind of compassion. It's a kind of friendship. You use the word love. Maybe it's God's word, given to you to use. Enough said. I know this much, old man, today, tomorrow, one day, you will have to stop sleeping with one eye open. Enough said really.

JONAH *goes to the pram.*

OTTO. I could have given you a beer. Or some cider.

JONAH *puts Ginny in the pram.*

JONAH. I can't drink because of the birds.

*He adjusts Ginny's covers. He looks at* OTTO.

I don't want anything.

OTTO *walks somewhere.*

OTTO. I wish you would want something.

OTTO *stops.*

I walk for walking's sake sometimes. To be alone.

JONAH. You should paint. I don't mean your living room, by the way.

OTTO. I'll think about it.

JONAH. You should.

OTTO. Yes.

JONAH. You won't.

OTTO. I will.

JONAH. You should retire and paint.

OTTO. I'll think about it.

JONAH. I hope you do.

OTTO. It's on the agenda.

JONAH. It's not.

OTTO. It is.

*A slight pause.*

I will think about it. I do think about it.

JONAH *speaks quietly.*

JONAH. Listen.

OTTO. What?

JONAH. Silence.

*A slight pause.*

Hang on. I can hear you thinking. It's time you stopped.

OTTO *chuckles.*

OTTO. You're the thick one.

JONAH. Yes. You should see my brother.

OTTO. What's he like?

JONAH. Clever.

OTTO. Your sister?

JONAH. She's just crazy like me.

OTTO *looks at his wrist.*

OTTO. Can I get you some cigarettes?

JONAH. I don't smoke.

OTTO. Because of the birds?

JONAH. Yes. Do me a favour. Paint the birds.

OTTO. I will.

JONAH. It's a promise.

OTTO. Yes.

*A slight pause.*

JONAH. If you want to know what they are. You're listening to
them now.

*A slight pause.*

OTTO. All I can hear is my tinnitus.

JONAH. Then you're not listening enough.

*A slight pause.*

OTTO. You're fucking enigmatic.

JONAH. Of course. I'm God.

OTTO *chuckles.*

OTTO. You bastard.

JONAH. You love it.

OTTO *looks at his wrist.*

OTTO. I hope you have a safe journey.

JONAH. We will.

OTTO. Give my love to France when you get there.

JONAH. Which bit?

OTTO. All of it. Go to the Louvre in Paris and look at any of the paintings, and think what those painters knew.

JONAH. All right.

OTTO. Think of an old cuckolder sometimes in England.

JONAH. I will.

OTTO. Think of life. Won't you?

JONAH. Of course.

*The town-hall clock, nearby, strikes ten o'clock.*

*The moon is high. The shadows have gone.*

*On the last stroke of ten,* JONAH *takes hold of the pram and starts to exit. He stops. He turns.*

See you. Thanks.

OTTO. Bye, Jonah.

JONAH *exits with the pram.*

*A slight pause.*

OTTO *goes to the wall. He takes the jacket off the nail and folds it over his arm.*

*An orange comes tumbling across the ground from the direction* JONAH *left in.* OTTO *bends down and stops it. He picks it up. He looks at it for a moment and puts it in his pocket. He exits the other way to* JONAH.

*The End.*